This Log book
Belongs to

_____

_____

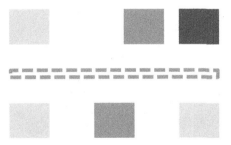

Date   Month   Week   Year

#	Item	Qty	Expiry Date

Date	Month	Week	Year

#	Item	Qty	Expiry Date

Date _____ Month _____ Week _____ Year _____

#	Item	Qty	Expiry Date

Date   Month   Week   Year

#	Item	Qty	Expiry Date

Date _ _ _ _ Month _ _ _ _ Week _ _ _ _ Year _ _ _ _

#	Item	Qty	Expiry Date

Date _ _ _ _ Month _ _ _ _ Week _ _ _ _ Year _ _ _ _

#	Item	Qty	Expiry Date

Date   Month   Week   Year

#	Item	Qty	Expiry Date

Date   Month   Week   Year

#	Item	Qty	Expiry Date

Date   Month   Week   Year

#	Item	Qty	Expiry Date

#	Item	Qty	Expiry Date

Date _____ Month _____ Week _____ Year _____

#	Item	Qty	Expiry Date

Date   Month   Week   Year

#	Item	Qty	Expiry Date

#	Item	Qty	Expiry Date

Date _____ Month _____ Week _____ Year _____

#	Item	Qty	Expiry Date

#	Item	Qty	Expiry Date

Date   Month   Week   Year

#	Item	Qty	Expiry Date

Date   Month   Week   Year

#	Item	Qty	Expiry Date

Date   Month   Week   Year

#	Item	Qty	Expiry Date

Date	Month	Week	Year

#	Item	Qty	Expiry Date

#	Item	Qty	Expiry Date

Date   Month   Week   Year

#	Item	Qty	Expiry Date

#	Item	Qty	Expiry Date

Date ____ Month ____ Week ____ Year ____

#	Item	Qty	Expiry Date

#	Item	Qty	Expiry Date

Date   Month   Week   Year

#	Item	Qty	Expiry Date

Date   Month   Week   Year

#	Item	Qty	Expiry Date

Date _____ Month _____ Week _____ Year _____

#	Item	Qty	Expiry Date

Date   Month   Week   Year

#	Item	Qty	Expiry Date

Date   Month   Week   Year

#	Item	Qty	Expiry Date

#	Item	Qty	Expiry Date

Date _ _ _ _ _ _ Month _ _ _ _ _ _ Week _ _ _ _ _ _ Year _ _ _ _ _ _

#	Item	Qty	Expiry Date

| Date | Month | Week | Year |

#	Item	Qty	Expiry Date

Date   Month   Week   Year

#	Item	Qty	Expiry Date

#	Item	Qty	Expiry Date

Date		Month		Week		Year

#	Item	Qty	Expiry Date

| Date | Month | Week | Year |

#	Item	Qty	Expiry Date

Date   Month   Week   Year

#	Item	Qty	Expiry Date

Date _____ Month _____ Week _____ Year _____

#	Item	Qty	Expiry Date

Date ─ ─ ─ Month ─ ─ ─ Week ─ ─ ─ Year ─ ─ ─ ─ ─ ─ ─ ─ ─ ─ ─ ─

#	Item	Qty	Expiry Date

Date	Month	Week	Year

#	Item	Qty	Expiry Date

#	Item	Qty	Expiry Date

Date _____ Month _____ Week _____ Year _____

#	Item	Qty	Expiry Date

Date	Month	Week	Year

#	Item	Qty	Expiry Date

Date _ _ _ Month _ _ _ Week _ _ _ Year _ _ _

#	Item	Qty	Expiry Date

Date   Month   Week   Year

#	Item	Qty	Expiry Date

Date _____ Month _____ Week _____ Year _____

#	Item	Qty	Expiry Date

#	Item	Qty	Expiry Date

#	Item	Qty	Expiry Date

Date   Month   Week   Year
- -

#	Item	Qty	Expiry Date

Date   Month   Week   Year

#	Item	Qty	Expiry Date

#	Item	Qty	Expiry Date

Date _____ Month _____ Week _____ Year _____

#	Item	Qty	Expiry Date

Date _ _ _ _ _ Month _ _ _ _ _ Week _ _ _ _ _ Year _ _ _ _ _ _ _

#	Item	Qty	Expiry Date

#	Item	Qty	Expiry Date

#	Item	Qty	Expiry Date

#	Item	Qty	Expiry Date

#	Item	Qty	Expiry Date

Date   Month   Week   Year

#	Item	Qty	Expiry Date

Date   Month   Week   Year

#	Item	Qty	Expiry Date

Date	Month	Week	Year

#	Item	Qty	Expiry Date

Date _____ Month _____ Week _____ Year _____

#	Item	Qty	Expiry Date

Date   Month   Week   Year

#	Item	Qty	Expiry Date

Date _____ Month _____ Week _____ Year _____

#	Item	Qty	Expiry Date

Date   Month   Week   Year

#	Item	Qty	Expiry Date

Date _ _ _ Month _ _ _ Week _ _ _ Year _ _ _

#	Item	Qty	Expiry Date

#	Item	Qty	Expiry Date

#	Item	Qty	Expiry Date

Date .... Month .... Week .... Year ....

#	Item	Qty	Expiry Date

Date   Month   Week   Year

#	Item	Qty	Expiry Date

Date	Month	Week	Year

#	Item	Qty	Expiry Date

#	Item	Qty	Expiry Date

Date _ _ _ Month _ _ _ Week _ _ _ Year

#	Item	Qty	Expiry Date

Date _ _ _ _ Month _ _ _ _ Week _ _ _ _ Year _ _ _ _

#	Item	Qty	Expiry Date

Date	Month	Week	Year

#	Item	Qty	Expiry Date

#	Item	Qty	Expiry Date

#	Item	Qty	Expiry Date

| Date | Month | Week | Year |

#	Item	Qty	Expiry Date

| Date | Month | Week | Year |

#	Item	Qty	Expiry Date

#	Item	Qty	Expiry Date

Date   Month   Week   Year

#	Item	Qty	Expiry Date

Date _____ Month _____ Week _____ Year _____

#	Item	Qty	Expiry Date

Date ____ Month ____ Week ____ Year ____

#	Item	Qty	Expiry Date

Date ___ Month ___ Week ___ Year ___

#	Item	Qty	Expiry Date

Date _____ Month _____ Week _____ Year _____

#	Item	Qty	Expiry Date

| Date | Month | Week | Year |

#	Item	Qty	Expiry Date

Date	Month	Week	Year

#	Item	Qty	Expiry Date

Date   Month   Week   Year

#	Item	Qty	Expiry Date

#	Item	Qty	Expiry Date

| Date | Month | Week | Year |

#	Item	Qty	Expiry Date

Date   Month   Week   Year

#	Item	Qty	Expiry Date

Date   Month   Week   Year

#	Item	Qty	Expiry Date

Date	Month	Week	Year

#	Item	Qty	Expiry Date

Date   Month   Week   Year

#	Item	Qty	Expiry Date

Date	Month	Week	Year

#	Item	Qty	Expiry Date

Date   Month   Week   Year

#	Item	Qty	Expiry Date

Date   Month   Week   Year

#	Item	Qty	Expiry Date

Date   Month   Week   Year

#	Item	Qty	Expiry Date

Date   Month   Week   Year

#	Item	Qty	Expiry Date

| Date | Month | Week | Year |

#	Item	Qty	Expiry Date

| Date | Month | Week | Year |

#	Item	Qty	Expiry Date

Date   Month   Week   Year

#	Item	Qty	Expiry Date

Date   Month   Week   Year

#	Item	Qty	Expiry Date

Date   Month   Week   Year

#	Item	Qty	Expiry Date

Date - - - - - Month - - - - - Week - - - - - Year - - - - -

#	Item	Qty	Expiry Date

Date   Month   Week   Year

#	Item	Qty	Expiry Date

#	Item	Qty	Expiry Date

Date   Month   Week   Year

#	Item	Qty	Expiry Date

Date ___ Month ___ Week ___ Year ___

#	Item	Qty	Expiry Date

Date _ _ _ Month _ _ _ Week _ _ _ Year _ _ _

#	Item	Qty	Expiry Date

| Date | Month | Week | Year |

#	Item	Qty	Expiry Date

#	Item	Qty	Expiry Date

Date	Month	Week	Year

#	Item	Qty	Expiry Date

Date   Month   Week   Year

#	Item	Qty	Expiry Date

Date   Month   Week   Year

#	Item	Qty	Expiry Date

#	Item	Qty	Expiry Date

#	Item	Qty	Expiry Date

Date   Month   Week   Year

#	Item	Qty	Expiry Date

Date   Month   Week   Year

#	Item	Qty	Expiry Date